From the desktop of Jeffrey Simmons

A vacation in Paris inspired Miroslav Sasek to create childrens travel guides to the big cities of the world. He brought me *This is Paris* in 1958 when I was publishing in London, and we soon followed up with *This is London.* Both books were enormously successful, and his simple vision grew to include more than a dozen books. Their amusing verse, coupled with bright and charming illustrations, made for a series unlike any other, and garnered Sasek (as we always called him) the international and popular acclaim he deserved.

I was thrilled to learn that *This is Israel* will once again find its rightful place on book-shelves. Sasek is no longer with us (and I have lost all contact with his family), but I am sure he would be delighted to know that a whole new generation of wide-eyed readers is being introduced to his whimsical, imaginative, and enchanting world.

Your name here

Published by arrangement with Simon & Schuster Books for Young Readers,
Simon & Schuster Children's Publishing Division

This edition first published in the United States of America in 2008 by
UNIVERSE PUBLISHING
A Division of Rizzoli International Publications, Inc.
300 Park Avenue South
New York, NY 10010
www.rizzoliusa.com

*See updated Israel facts at end of book

2008 2009 2010 2011 2012 / 10 9 8 7 6 5 4 3 2 1

Printed in China

ISBN 10: 0-7893-1595-5
ISBN 13: 978-0-7893-1595-3

Library of Congress Control Number: 2007934237

Cover design: centerpointdesign

M. Sasek

This is
ISRAEL

UNIVERSE

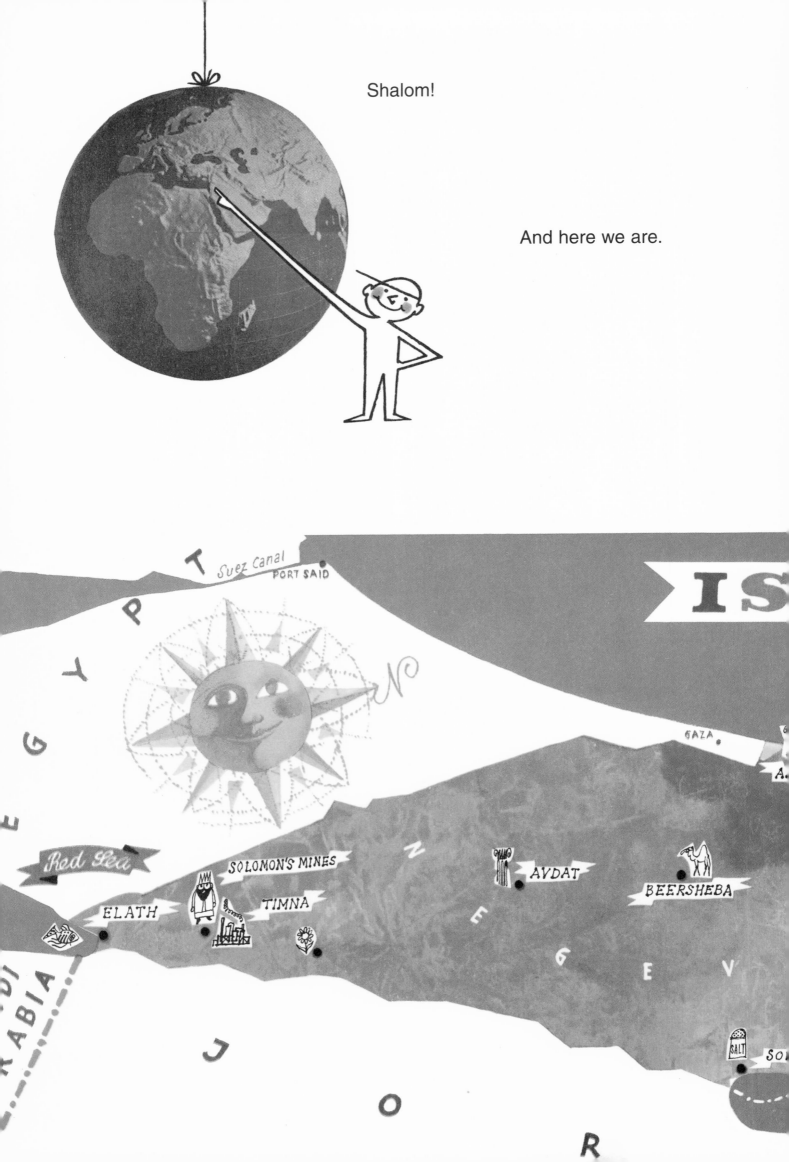

Shalom!

And here we are.

As you can see, we are not in a huge country. It is no bigger than Wales, or the state of New Jersey. But it is a Promised Land and a land of promise. It is the land of the Bible.

"And see the land, what it is; and the people that dwelleth therein."

(NUMBERS 13:18)

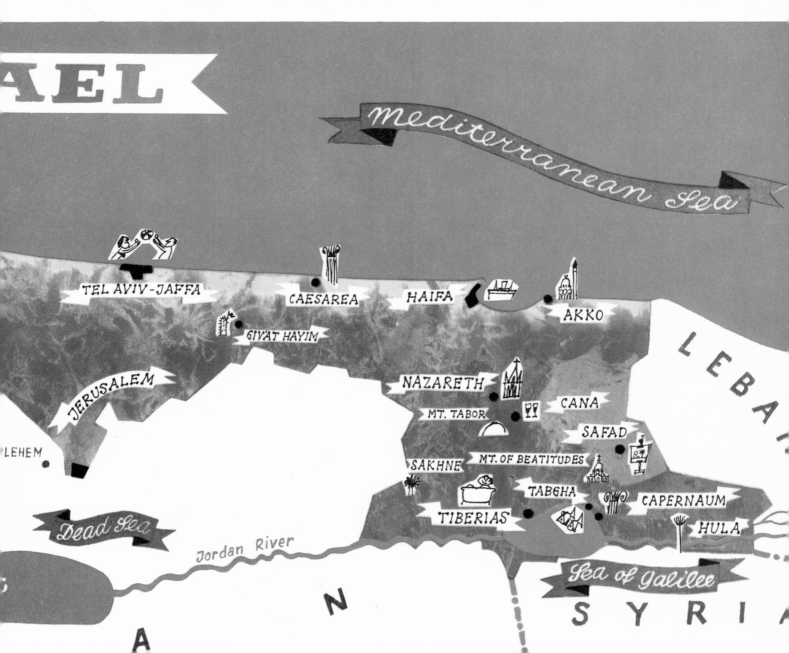

"A land of wheat, and barley, and vines, and fig trees, and pomegranates; a land of oil olive, and honey."

(DEUTERONOMY 8:8)

Valley of Jezreel

A land of oranges

9

Sakhne at the foot of Mount Gilboa

"A land of brooks of water, of fountains and depths that spring out of valleys and hills."

(DEUTERONOMY 8:7)

Papyrus in the Hula Valley in Upper Galilee*

King Solomon's Mines at Timna

Modern Timna, just one hill away

"A land whose stones are iron, and out of whose hills thou mayest dig brass."

(DEUTERONOMY 8:9)

A land from whose soil thou mayest also dig historic cities.

Caesarea — ancient capital of Roman Palestine

Avdat — ancient caravan crossroads of the Nabateans in the central Negev

Ashkelon — ancient Philistine city, birthplace of Herod,

Giv'at Hayim

A land of the kibbutz

A land whose four foreign borders have only a single crossing-point: the Mandelbaum gate in Jerusalem*

A land without Israeli TV stations —

but Sheikh Sulleman may look at Arabic TV from Cairo and Beirut, and tourists may look at Sheikh Sulleman's complex aerial and at his Bedouins.*

17

AS A ROARING LION,
AND A RANGING BEAR;
SO IS A WICKED RULER
OVER THE POOR PEOPLE.
(PROV. 28 :15)

A land where you can brush up on your Bible even in the zoo

Bibles and Boeings

Camels and Cadillacs

People from a hundred countries —

More than five million Jews and almost a million and a half Muslims, Christians, and Druzes —

different beard-do's

different tongues

different customs.

A native-born Israeli is called a "sabra"
after the prickly pear or fruit of the cactus.
Both are supposed to be sweet inside.

Different kinds of business

from coffee to toffee-apples

The colorful market in Akko

The old Synagogue Ha'ari in Safed

24

Different religions:

Safed, once a home of Jewish mysticism, today
a home of the arts

The Franciscan Church on the Mount of the Beatitudes,
where Jesus preached the Sermon on the Mount.

25

In Akko — once a Phoenician port, and later a stronghold of the Crusaders —

stands the famous Mosque of El-Jazzar Pasha.

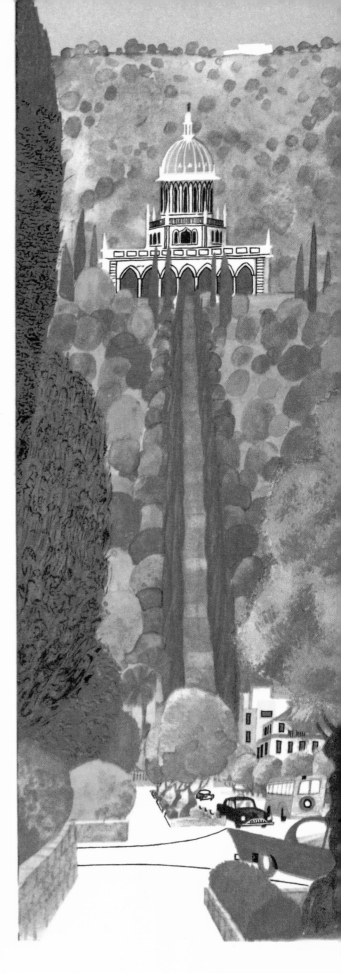

In Haifa — the Baha'i Shrine where Bab, the founder of the Baha'i faith, is buried.

Tel Aviv-Jaffa, with its 380,000 inhabitants, is the second largest city in Israel.

Tel Aviv was founded in 1909 as

a suburb of Jaffa.

The biblical city of Joppa (called Jaffa today) was thought to have been built by Japhet, the son of Noah.

The Habimah National Theatre

The Frederic Mann Concert Hall

Tel Aviv entertains.

Haifa works.

It is the main port of Israel.

The Bay of Haifa seen from Mount Carmel, where
Elijah confounded the prophets of Baal

The Hebrew University campus

Jerusalem studies and prays.

The building of the Chief Rabbinate — the supreme religious authority in the country

Jerusalem, city of David, capital of Israel, spiritual home of the Jewish people

The Old City and its shrines belong to Jordan,

but Mount Zion, "beautiful for situation, the joy of
the whole earth" (Psalms 48:2), holy to Jews,
Christians, and Muslims, is in Israel.*

Here you can visit the Tomb of King David, the Room of the
Last Supper, and the Dormition Abbey.

The Mount of Olives

King David's Tomb

The Room of the Last Supper

Nazareth, where "Jesus increased in wisdom and stature, and in favour with God and man" (ST. LUKE 2:52). It has Israel's largest Arab-Christian population. The Basilica of the Annunciation in Nazareth is the goal of Christian pilgrims from all over the world.

St. Mary's Well*

This is where the Holy Family lived after their return from Egypt.

A different kind of housing awaits new arrivals in Nazareth.

Leading from Nazareth, the roads of Galilee are
roads of the Gospels and of Jesus' miracles:

Cana of Galilee, where water became wine —

Capernaum, where the centurion's servant was healed —

Tabgha, where a few loaves and fishes fed multitudes —

שרידי בית-מרחץ
מהתקופה ההרודינית- רומית במאה הראשונה
RUINS OF BATH HOUSE
of the HERODIAN ROMAN PERIOD 1st Cent C.E

Tiberias, 682 feet below sea level, a resort founded by Herod Antipas (son of Herod the Great) to the glory of the Roman emperor Tiberius, who enjoyed bathing here in the hot springs

The River Jordan connects the Sea of Galilee with the Dead Sea.

This is the road to the Dead Sea.

Sodom, the lowest point on dry land in the world, 1,292 feet below sea level. Swimmers in the Dead Sea cannot sink: its 32 percent salt content supports them — and a thriving chemical industry.*

Here is Lot's wife, a pillar of salt.

Beersheba, once the home of Abraham and his family, now the "capital" of the Negev Desert, a gold-rush city where "gold" means the minerals of the desert and the Dead Sea

It is a city of research where solar rays are
set to heating water —

and producing energy.

Once a week there is a Bedouin market in Beersheba —

where you can buy a racing camel for the price of a car.

You can roadtest your camel before closing the deal.

On the Red Sea at Israel's southernmost tip lies Eilat, her gateway to
Africa and Asia.

The Red Sea is blue. Its fishes can be studied by tourists through
the floors of the glass-bottomed boats —

and vice versa.

Between Eilat and Beersheba stretches the Negev Desert, geographically more than half of all Israel. Silence, loneliness, wilderness, the end of the world.*

But it is also a beginning:

Kibbutz Yotvata in the middle of nowhere —

where small "sabras" play and grow up —

their parents work in the fields* —

and "The wilderness and the solitary place shall be glad
for them; and the desert shall rejoice, and blossom . . . " (ISAIAH 35:1)

THIS IS ISRAEL . . . TODAY!

*Page 11: In the 1950s, Lake Hula in the Hula Valley was drained in order to provide agricultural land and to destroy the breeding ground of a malaria-carrying mosquito. A small area of papyrus swampland was set aside, which eventually became Israel's first nature reserve. In 1994, in an attempt to restore additional natural habitat that was destroyed by the drainage project, a large portion of the valley was re-flooded, creating Lake Agmon. Within the first several years, 74 plant species colonized the wetland spontaneously and 120 species of birds have been recorded in or around the lake.

*Page 17: Following the Six Day War in June 1967, in which Israeli forces captured Jerusalem, the Mandelbaum Gate (which was in fact not a gate but merely a passage between barbed wire entanglements) was torn down. Today only a historical marker remains.

*Page 17: The Israeli government authorized television in 1967 and the first shows were aired two years later. Today there are state-managed and privately-owned stations, as well as cable, satellite, and Arabic TV.

*Page 36: Following the 1948 Arab-Israeli War, Jerusalem was divided into two parts: the western portion, populated mainly by Jews, came under Israeli sovereignty, while the eastern portion (including the Old City), populated mainly by Arabs, came under Jordanian rule. After the 1967 Six Day War, the eastern part of Jerusalem came under Israeli rule and was merged with the western municipality.

*Page 42: St. Mary's Well is the site of the Annunciation, where the angel Gabriel appeared to Mary and announced that she would give birth to the son of God.

*Page 48: The famously salty sea is shrinking. As a result of river diversions, mineral extraction, and natural reasons like evaporation, it has been receding by roughly three feet a year for the past 25 years. Experts predict that unless water levels are boosted, the Dead Sea and its unique ecosystem could vanish by 2050.

*Page 56: Although the Negev constitutes 60 percent of Israel's land mass, just 8 percent of the population calls it home (mostly Bedouins and other nomadic groups). To relieve congestion and overcrowding in central Israel, the government has recently undertaken an ambitious plan to develop this vast region.

*Page 60: At most modern kibbutzim, members are engaged in much more than field work. At Yotvata, for example, there is a dairy plant, a restaurant, several cottage industries such as jewelry-making and blacksmithing, and a variety of international educational projects.